STREET SMARTS

Activities That Help Teenagers Take Care of Themselves

Dr. Michael Kirby

Resource Publications, Inc.
San Jose, California

Editorial director: Kenneth Guentert
Managing editor: Elizabeth J. Asborno
Editorial assistant: Cindy Tolliver

Reprint Department
Resource Publications, Inc.
160 E. Virginia Street #290
San Jose, CA 95112-5876

Library of Congress Cataloging in Publication Data
available.

Printed in the United States of America

99 98 97 96 95 | 5 4 3 2 1

*This curriculum was originally published in the United
Kingdom as* Streetwise: Education for Citizenship © *1993
Daniels Publishing.*

Contents

Introduction

T his resource examines a range of social problems that can affect young people (ages fourteen to nineteen) as they make the transition from the relatively secure environments of home and school to the world of work and adulthood.

Each chapter covers essential information about the problem topic, analyzes causes and consequences, and provides a wide range of related activities. Case studies and role-play exercises illustrate key points and stimulate the active involvement of young people in the learning process.

English, social science, sociology, career preparation, and other courses of study can incorporate this material. Other applications include courses and discussion groups organized by youth workers, health education instructors, and others responsible for the welfare and training of young people. The main goals of *Street Smarts* are:

- to promote awareness among young people of problems that particularly affect their age group

- to encourage them to develop positive attitudes about and solutions to these problems

The activities in this book are based on these objectives. You will find instructions for implementing each activity, but the activities are flexible enough for you to adapt them to suit your own requirements. For example, although each activity is earmarked for individual, small-group, or whole-group work, most of the activities will work in whatever way you want to present them. Whether your class works on the activities individually or in groups, in most cases you will want to invite the individuals or groups to report their findings and answers as part of a group discussion. Rather than looking for definitive answers, focus your discussion on why students answer as they do.

The restricted license to photocopy which accompanies this resource allows activity, role-play, and case study pages to be reproduced for each individual or small group in a class. Individual sheets can also be used with an overhead projector.

Consumer Issues

Before presenting this section, read over and decide which activities, role-plays, and/or case studies your class will do. Have photocopies of the selected pages ready to hand out.

Before the Second World War, very few goods and services were produced specifically for teenagers and young adults. Two main reasons for this were:

- Wages for young workers were generally low, so they had little spare cash for luxury items.

- Young people tended to spend their money on the same things as their parents and grandparents.

Since World War II, however, American companies have directed more and more of their marketing and sales efforts toward young people. This growth in the youth segment of the consumer market is due to three factors:

1. A sharp increase in the birth rate in post-war America meant that a record number of these so-called Baby Boomers would hit adolescence in the 1960s.

2. Youth culture emerged in the sixties as a major social force. These adolescents increasingly derived their values, tastes, and lifestyles from their peer group rather than from their elders.

3. Youth could back up their tastes with money. The new affluence of the fifties and sixties enabled parents to give their children allowances to spend on

themselves. Those young people with jobs were often allowed to spend their earnings as they pleased and didn't hand over their earnings to their families as they had in the past.

The result was that American youth controlled a substantial portion of the nation's discretionary income. This trend did not escape the notice of American businessmen, who directed ever-larger portions of their advertising budgets as the lucrative youth market. Products such as soft drinks, motorcycles, and blue jeans were repackaged to appeal specifically to youth. Demand in the record industry soared with the growing popularity of rock and pop music, and for the first time, the fashion industry was dominated by styles intended solely for the young.

Individual Activity

Hand out the activity page "Young People—A Target Market" to each student. Allow about ten minutes for them to complete it.

ACTIVITY: Young People—A Target Market

1. Make a list of products produced specifically for young people.

_____   _____

_____   _____

_____   _____

_____   _____

2. Make a list of television shows and commercials aimed at young viewers.

_____   _____

_____   _____

_____   _____

_____   _____

Advertising

Buying records, clothes, cosmetics, and other items is a normal pattern of behavior for young people. What youth spend their money on should be a matter of free choice; however, if they buy something they don't really want because they feel pressured by advertisements, they are being exploited, and companies that create the ads are making money at their expense.

Some people think that advertising is a form of exploitation. According to this view, the aim of advertising is to persuade people to want things that they would not otherwise consider buying. Not everyone agrees with this view, though, pointing out that advertising also provides useful information and promotes good public relations for large companies.

Clearly, advertisers seek to persuade people to buy their product or service. Their effectiveness in persuading a certain segment of the population to buy its product depends on its knowledge of that target audience. Advertisements to teenagers are often based on the following "typical" teenage characteristics:

- Young people—more than any other age group—worry about their looks. Advertisers take advantage of these anxieties to promote a wide range of products which are supposed to enhance attractiveness. Stereotype images of handsome young men and impossibly beautiful young women make the product they are selling seem "sexy." The idea is this: If you use our product, you will be as gorgeous as the perfect images you see in our ads.

- Young people like to mimic adult behavior. From an early age, children are often chided with comments like "Grow up" or "Don't be childish." This can create anxiety for young people who are no longer children but may not yet be accepted as adults. Smoking advertisements, for example, imply that by puffing at a cigarette young people can show the world that they are definitely adults who should be treated on equal terms and not talked down to. The same message can be seen in advertisements for alcoholic drinks, banking services, cosmetics, and hair products. Some recruitment advertisements aimed at young people, such as those for the armed services, also imply that by accepting the job you will be transformed into an adult.

- Young people worry about being accepted by peers. As parents become less of an influence, the importance of friends increases; this is reflected in advertisements suggesting that in order to be popular with peers a person should dress in a particular way, buy a particular brand of something, or read the latest teen magazine.

- Young people often have unrealistically high expectations of material success. They look forward to having successful careers as well as a good time outside work. Ads play on these expectations by defining the material standards that the "truly successful" enjoy: flashy sports cars, exotic travel, and dinner in fancy restaurants. Other advertisements, such as those for dance clubs and rock concerts, attempt to tell young people what they should be spending their money on in order to have a good time. These advertisement make it seem that people are missing out on an important part of being young if they don't buy these products or services.

Whole Group Activity

Brainstorm a list of well-known advertisements directed at young people. Consider newspaper, magazine, television, and radio ads. Taking each listed item in turn, discuss the following questions:

- At whom is the advertisement aimed?

- What message(s) does it communicate?

- What techniques are used to influence the viewer/reader?

- Are these techniques the same as those presented in class? If not, how do they differ?

Becoming Savvy Consumers

If individuals are strong-minded and aware of the techniques that advertisers use to sell products, they will probably not be unduly influenced by advertisements. But if they are naive and easily persuaded, they may find themselves spending money on unwanted or unnecessary items. Young people must realize that the money they earn can be important for their future happiness. Learning to spend money wisely now will allow them to save for major items later, such as a car, business, or home.

Because advertisers find it relatively easy to sell products and services to young people, they pay less attention to the quality of these products and services. If young people become more discriminating in how they spend their dollars, they become harder to sell to. This forces manufacturers to improve the quality of their products and services.

Small Group Activity

Ask the students to form small groups for the following activity. Allow about thirty minutes for them to finish, then ask each group to present the details of its advertisement to the whole class. The class should try to determine which techniques the advertisement is using to persuade its target audience.

ACTIVITY: Write Your Own Advertisement

Imagine that your advertising executives and you have been asked to produce a television commercial for one of the following products:

- expensive running shoes

- a new toothpaste that also acts as a breath freshener

- a vacation resort in Hawaii for eighteen to thirty year olds

Aim your advertisement at young people. Use the techniques presented in class. Discuss the details together, then use the space below to describe the advertisement and to explain why you think it would persuade young people to buy the product. You will need to be able to present your ideas to the whole class.

Your Rights As a Consumer

Although consumers expect products to be fairly priced, safe, and of reasonable quality, this is not always the case. When people are dissatisfied with a product or service, they can take various courses of action depending on the circumstances and how far they want to go in pursuing the complaint.

Talk to a Customer Service Person

In almost all cases, the sensible first step is to discuss the problem with a person in authority at the store where you purchased the item. Don't start off on the wrong foot by being aggressive or rude. In fact, try to remain calm and polite no matter what response you get from the person in the shop. This approach is by far the best way of securing a satisfactory outcome without having to take your complaint any further. You will need to provide the following:

- the receipt, or else the date of purchase
- reasons you are dissatisfied with the product
- the actions you would like the store to make to rectify the situation: refund, replace, or repair the item

Speak (or Write a Letter) to the Manager

If you are not happy with your initial contact with customer service, you could speak to a more senior person or make a formal complaint in writing to the manager or owner of the store. If the store is part of a chain, write to the customer complaints department at its main office or headquarters. Any letter should contain the information outlined above.

Contact the Nearest Better Business Bureau

Your local Better Business Bureau monitors the advertising and selling practices of businesses in most areas. They can help in the following ways:

- provide information about a specific company, including reliability reports
- assist with resolving a complaint against a business
- provide consumer education on products and services
- provide records of complaints

Investigate Consumer Protection Laws

Consumer protection laws at both the federal and state levels protect buyers from unfair business practices and from goods or services that fail to meet basic standards. In general, consumer protection laws do the following:

- require businesses to disclose important information about products, services, agreements, and credit terms

- prohibit businesses from using misleading or deceptive information or practices

- establish health, safety, and performance standards that spell out how safe products or services must be or how well they should perform

If you file a complaint against the supplier of a product or service and with the Better Business Bureau but are still unable to reach a satisfactory agreement, check to see if the law is on your side. Before taking on the expense of an attorney, contact the appropriate state or federal agency that enforces consumer law. Staff people will often provide free advice, answer general questions about the law, and might help you investigate your complaint. If you're not sure which agency you should contact, ask your local librarian for a listing of regulatory agencies. Such organizations include:

- federal agencies such as the Federal Trade commission (FTC) and the United States Office of Consumer Affairs (OCA)

- state consumer protection agencies and other regulatory organizations such as the insurance commission and utility department

- industry and business associations that monitor their own members, such as the retail or booksellers associations

Don't Give Up

In spite of a solid case against the supplier of a product or service, sometimes tenacious efforts are necessary to obtain satisfaction. Frequent visits to the store where you bought the item, writing several letters of complaint, or even threatening legal action as a last resort are often part of the process. Don't let any roadblocks store personnel or management throw in your path frustrate you to the point of settling for an unsatisfactory outcome.

Small Group Activity

Ask the class to form small groups for the activity "Grounds for Complaint?" Allow about ten to fifteen minutes to complete the handout.

When they have finished, go over their responses. Below are suggested answers to each situation.

1. Carol might well feel annoyed that she has paid more for the skirt, but she has no grounds for complaint because she knew the price of the skirt before she bought it and was happy to pay the price at that point. She could return to the store and point out that the same skirt is being offered for sale at half-price elsewhere in town, but the store would be under no obligation to take the skirt back or compensate Carol in any way.

2. Mark should file a complaint to the Better Business Bureau. After doing so, if he is still not satisfied, he could contact the state jeweler's association and try to have his jeweler's license suspended..

3. Dave probably does not have much of a case for complaint. The wrench was obviously a cheap make and he did get a few months' use out of it.

4. Sara has grounds for complaint. The heater was clearly not fit for its intended use. If not satisfied by the supplier, Sara should consult her local librarian to determine the appropriate consumer organization to contact.

5. Jenna, Clare, and Penny should complain. If there was a clear understanding with the travel agents through whom they booked the vacation that the suite would have an ocean view, a balcony, and three beds, they are entitled to compensation. If the travel agent won't give them a refund, they should complain to the Better Business Bureau. If that doesn't work, they can contact the state board that licenses travel agencies to file a complaint.

ACTIVITY: Grounds for Complaint?

The following people are dissatisfied with their purchases. In your small group, decide whether or not each person has any grounds for complaint and, if so, what action should be taken.

1. After buying a skirt for $25, Carol found that exact same skirt on sale in another store for $12.

2. Mark bought an expensive engagement ring for his girlfriend. Although the jeweler assured him that the band was 18-carat gold with a cluster of five diamonds, Mark subsequently discovered that the ring was only 9-carat gold and that there were six diamonds instead of five.

3. Dave bought a wrench so he could work on his motorcycle. Several wrenches were on sale at the hardware store, and he bought the least expensive one. After a few months' use, the wrench broke.

4. Sara purchased a new electric heater for her flat. The first time she switched it on, it sparked and then blew a fuse. Her brother, an electrician, confirmed that the heater is faulty.

5. Jenna, Clare, and Penny booked a vacation to Hawaii through their local travel agent. They were supposed to get a hotel suite with three beds and a balcony with an ocean view. When they arrived, they found only two beds and a view of the parking lot.

Small Group Role-Play

Ask the class to form groups of three. Allow about fifteen minutes for the groups to compose a three-minute role-play, which they will present to the whole class.

Afterward, ask the Sams whether they found it easy to argue their case with the store manager and clerk.

Compile a list of the main arguments each character in each group used, then ask the groups to choose what they consider the best two arguments from each side.

ROLE-PLAY: A Matter of Sole

Background Information

Sam bought a pair of expensive brand-name running shoes from a local sporting goods store. After wearing them a few times, the soles started to split and come away from the rest of the shoe. Though Sam lost the receipt, he took the shoes back to the store to complain and ask for a refund. However, the store manager was reluctant to give him a refund, and the clerk who served Sam claimed not to remember selling the trainers to Sam.

Three-Minute Role-Play

Base your role-play on the scene in the shop as Sam tries to persuade the manager and the clerk to take the shoes back and give him a refund. Sam should state his case clearly and not back down. The manager and the clerk should deny responsibility and argue why they will not accept Sam's complaint. Eventually, though, the manager should give in and agree to offer Sam a refund.

2 *Cults*

Before presenting this section, read over and decide which activities, role-plays, and/or case studies your class will do. Have photocopies of the selected pages ready to hand out.

Cults and their members are making the news more often lately. Details of these reports vary, but often they focus on a young person who left home to join a cult, causing great distress to his/her friends and relatives. Other elements of the typical media story include:

- an accusation that the young person has been brainwashed into joining the cult

- an accusation that the cult is turning the person against his/her parents

- a presentation of the cult's behavior as weird and threatening to the values of society

- an assumption that the young person would like to return home to a "normal" life if only he/she were free to choose

According to the *Random House Dictionary of the English Language* (2nd ed. unabridged, New York, 1987), a cult is a "particular system of religious worship, esp. with reference to its rites and ceremonies." This rather broad definition could easily apply to all religions. More often today we use the word "cult" to refer to a particular type of religious worship. Usually, cults have the following features:

- They are small religious groups whose activities are regarded as unconventional by mainstream society.

- They are new religions. Though cults may share some beliefs in common with world religions such as Christianity or Islam, their beliefs and practices differ radically from those of the established churches.

- They require intense loyalty and personal sacrifice from their followers.

- Rituals and ceremonies are crucial to the identity of the cult.

- Their spiritual leaders, and often their followers, have withdrawn from the wider society and are critical of its materialistic values.

Popular cults in the media include: Hare Krishna, Unification Church (the Moonies), the Happy-Healthy-Holy Organization, Children of God, Scientologists, and the Jesus Movement.

Sometimes the word "cult" is used to describe non-religious groups which nevertheless have some of the characteristics of a religion. For example, fans of heavy metal music are sometimes referred to as a cult because of their slavish devotion to this type of music and idol worship of the musicians.

Individual Activity

Hand out the activity page "Why Join a Cult?" and allow about ten minutes for the students to complete it. Invite students to share their answers.

ACTIVITY: Why Join a Cult?

Here is a list of factors contributing to why a person might join a cult. Choose three and explain why that factor might lead to joining a cult.

- Boredom
- Depression
- Desire to be different
- Loneliness
- Lack of meaning in one's life
- Death of a parent
- Desire to "get back at" a relative or friend

Small Group Role-Play

Ask the class to form groups of four. Hand out the role-play to each group, and give them about twenty-five minutes to create a five-minute role-play.

Each group should present its role-play to the whole class. Afterward, discuss as a class whether Susan and her parents could recover their relationship.

ROLE-PLAY: Joining a Cult

Background Information

Susan, nineteen, left home last year to go to college. During her first term, followers of a cult approached her and she joined the group to find out more about its beliefs. Her parents became worried when she didn't return home during Christmas vacation, choosing instead to spend the time with other followers of the cult at their country retreat. Susan didn't return to college for the next term but remained at the retreat. Now she writes to her parents but refuses to see them. She tells them that the cult's followers are her new family. Susan's parents cannot believe that their daughter is choosing not to see them and think that she must have been brainwashed. A close family friend has offered to visit Susan at the retreat, but not until she hears what Susan's parents think has happened to her.

Five-Minute Role-Play

Decide who will play the Friend, the Father, the Mother, and Susan. The role-play is in two parts:

1. Start with the scene where the Friend discusses with Susan's parents what has happened to cause such a change in their daughter. Try to imagine how the parents feel and express this in the way you play the roles. The Friend should listen sympathetically, occasionally asking questions to get more information from the parents about why they think their daughter has been brainwashed.

2. The second part of the role-play focuses on the meeting between Susan and the Friend. The role of the Friend is to explain to Susan how her parents feel about the situation and what they think has happened to her. She also wants to hear what Susan has to say. Her main concern is to persuade Susan that she is not taking sides and that she has an open mind about what has happened. She hasn't come to the retreat to take Susan away against her will; she just wants to see if she can help Susan and her parents reach a better understanding of what has happened to their relationship.

Whoever plays the role of Susan should decide whether Susan is in fact the brainwashed person her parents think she is or an independent-minded young adult with reasons of her own why she wants to stay with the cult.

Small Group Case Study

Ask the class to form small groups and hand out the following case study to each group. One member should read the Background Information, then the members of the group should discuss the accompanying questions. Allow about thirty minutes for the entire exercise.

CASE STUDY: Joe

Background Information

Joe hadn't given much thought to religion before Lesley and Paul approached him in the park. His mother used to go to church, but he never knew whether she really believed in it. He thought she probably went because it was the "in thing" in their town. Anyway, her religion didn't stop her from running off with another man when Joe was only ten, leaving his dad to raise three school-age children alone.

At eighteen, Joe was unemployed; though he used to spend a couple of hours each morning working out at a local gym where he belonged to an amateur boxing club, not much seemed to be happening in his life. He had left home a few weeks earlier, and even though one of his friend's mother let him sleep over, she didn't like him staying in the house during the day when they were out. So he spent most of his time hanging around town.

Lesley and Paul, on the other hand, smiled a lot and looked as if they were having a good time. They explained that they were from a center in town where young people could meet and talk about life and the things that mattered to them. Joe wasn't used to people being so friendly. When they invited him to come back to the center, he accepted because he didn't want to disappoint them. Anyway, he couldn't think of anything better to do that day.

The center was warm and even provided free coffee and snacks. No one told him what to do or gave him a hassle. Everyone was friendly and had time to talk. Discussion meetings at lunchtime were well-attended. Joe didn't feel left out, though, because they were so friendly, and he didn't have to say anything unless he wanted to.

Sometimes Lesley or Paul stood up and talked about why the center existed and what they believed in. According to them, the center was an example of how people could live together in harmony and peace through love and sharing,. Most of the world didn't live like this; society encouraged people to be greedy and competitive. The world would have to undergo a big change in order to make people see that they are capable of real love for each other. Lesley and Paul belonged to a movement trying to achieve this kind of change.

CASE STUDY: Joe (page 2)

After Joe had been to the center a few times, Lesley and Paul asked if he would like to spend a weekend as their guest at a house in the country where followers from across the nation met to discuss their beliefs. It would be a chance for him to find out more about the movement without being committed to join. They offered to pay for Joe's expenses and they even gave him some money to buy new clothes.

The weekend was different from what Joe expected. Right from the start, he was asked to join in with singing, prayers, and discussions that went on all day and into the night. The cult included elements from Buddhism and Christianity in their teachings. They believed that Jesus was sent by God to redeem the world but that he was only partially successful in his mission. He had established a spiritual kingdom, but the task of bringing about the physical kingdom of God on earth was yet to be accomplished. Their task was to bring the world to recognize that God was in the hands of their leader, the new Messiah, who could establish the kingdom with the aid of devoted followers who have committed themselves to a rigorous life service.

It wasn't the greatest weekend Joe ever spent. With his senses dulled by lack of sleep and the constant bombardment of prayers and ideas, he went away undecided about whether to join the movement. But once he started thinking it over, he began to admire the followers for being so devoted. They got excited all right, but that was just their way of preparing to do a really difficult job. For Joe, it was similar to getting psyched up before stepping into the boxing ring. The followers weren't like his mother, who said she believed in God but never did anything about it.

The center meant a great deal to Joe, and Lesley and Paul were especially nice. They were probably the best friends he would ever had. So, Joe agreed to spend another weekend at the house in the country, and a few months later he became a follower. He worked for the movement full-time, lived in communes, and broke all ties with his family. Money he earned went to the movement.

CASE STUDY: Joe (page 3)

Discussion Questions

Discuss the following questions. Once your group agrees on an answer, write it down and be prepared to share it with the whole class.

1. Suggest three things about Joe's personality and circumstances that might explain why he was a likely candidate to be recruited by this cult.

2. What did Joe like about the center?

3. What persuaded Joe to join the cult?

4. Choose two excerpts from Joe's story that illustrate the techniques that cults use to attract young people to join.

5. Is there any evidence that the cult was trying to brainwash Joe? Support your answer.

6. By joining the cult, do you think Joe will be a happier person? Why or why not?

Becoming a Follower

Ultimately, the decision to join a religious cult is made by the individual. Accusations that followers are brainwashed into joining cults or are abducted and held against their will are exaggerated. However, becoming a cult follower is different from joining, say, a club or charity. It is likely to have a fundamental effect on the new member's life, and with some cults, it may mean being encouraged to limit contact with friends and relatives.

As you present the following, invite student feedback. Do they agree? Can they add other ideas?

Joining a cult is not a decision to take lightly. Some points worth bearing in mind for anyone who might be considering joining one are:

- Take time to find out about the cult before you make a decision, and don't allow anyone to pressure you into joining the cult.

- Reflect on your state of mind and personal circumstances at the time. If you are not your usual self or are experiencing special difficulties in your life, it might not be a good time to make a decision which could have far-reaching consequences for you and for your friends and relatives.

- Discuss the issues with someone who can offer good advice—a teacher, friend, relative, priest, counselor, etc.

- Be wary of the techniques which some cults use to persuade people to become followers. These techniques can range from crude attempts at brainwashing to quite subtle approaches such as offering friendship and emotional support to people in order to win their confidence and encourage them to think positively about the cult.

- If you join a cult, avoid losing complete contact with friends and relatives because you may need their help and support should you decide to leave the cult and rejoin mainstream society.

3 *Delinquency*

Before presenting this section, read over and decide which activities, role-plays, and/or case studies your class will do. Have photocopies of the selected pages ready to hand out.

Delinquency" is a term which describes law-breaking, whether committed by an adult or young person. "Juvenile delinquency" refers to any violation of the law by someone less than eighteen years old.

National concern is growing about the escalation of violent juvenile crime. The FBI reports that, over the past few years, juveniles were responsible for approximately sixteen percent of all arrests. Juveniles were involved in fifteen percent of murder arrests, sixteen percent of rape, twenty-six percent of robbery, fifteen percent of aggravated assault, thirty-four percent of burglary, forty-four percent of motor vehicle theft, twenty-three percent of weapons violations, and twenty-three percent of drug law violation. In general, eighty percent of delinquency cases involve males.

Although the public concern is primarily focused on the increase in violent juvenile crime, national trends also indicate that young people themselves are disproportionately the *victims* of juvenile crimes. America's youth are being killed in record numbers. Teenage boys from all racial and ethnic backgrounds are more likely to die from gunshot wounds than from all natural deaths combined. Perhaps the single most important impact on youth violence has been the increased availability of firearms.

Hand out the following activity page, and allow about ten minutes for the students to complete it.

ACTIVITY: Delinquency

1. Vandalism is one type of criminal offense which a young person might commit. List three other types of offense associated with young offenders.

2. Suggest two reasons why a young person might become a criminal.

3. Suggest two reasons why females who commit crimes might have a better chance of getting away with it than other groups.

Possible Reasons for Delinquency

According to the Department of Justice, certain factors tend to increase the risk of delinquent behavior:

- birth trauma
- child abuse and neglect
- ineffective parental discipline
- family disruptions
- conduct disorder and hyperactivity in children
- school failure
- learning disabilities
- negative peer influences
- limited employment opportunities
- inadequate housing
- residence in high-crime neighborhoods

Even though many adolescents are at high risk for delinquency, many never commit crimes. A host of factors related to the family, peer, and community environments help protect young people from engaging in negative behaviors. Parental supervision, closeness to parents, and consistency in discipline are the most important family factors. Commitment to school and the avoidance of delinquent and drug-using peers also help young people to avoid delinquency.

Whole Group Discussion

Invite the students to offer their ideas in answer to the following questions:

- Why do some adolescents commit crimes and not others?
- Why do more males than females commit crimes?

Individual Activity

Hand out the following activity page, and allow about fifteen minutes for students to write their reports.

Invite one or two students to read their reports, and have the class discuss whether the details about Darren's background would contribute to his delinquency.

ACTIVITY: A Probation Officer's Perspective

Background Information

Darren is nineteen and has recently been arrested and charged with stealing VCRs and other electrical equipment from a local store. Two of Darren's friends have been charged with the same offense. This is not the first time Darren has been in trouble with the police.

Court Report

Imagine that you are a probation officer who has been asked to prepare a report to be read in court, giving details about Darren's background that might help explain why he has been in trouble so often with the police. You will have to make up the details, of course, but try to make them convincing. Include in your report something about Darren's family background, his education and employment record, his friends and lifestyle, etc.

Dealing with Crime

The following are a brief introduction to the options available to the authorities—the police and the courts—for dealing with offenders.

Keep in mind that because criminal codes vary from state to state, these are only general statements about law enforcement. You may want to research specific procedures in your state to supplement this discussion.

Warning

If the person has committed a minor offense and has not been in trouble with the authorities before, the police may simply give a warning. A record of the warning is kept in case the person commits any further crimes.

Court Appearance

If the police have sufficient evidence, they may decide to bring charges. The person concerned may be ticketed or arrested; either way, he/she will be ordered to appear in court. The two types of crimes a person can be tried for are misdemeanors and felonies; the type of crime a person commits determines the type of hearing he/she will have. Sometimes a case is transferred to criminal court so the juvenile may be tried as an adult. This decision is often based on the seriousness of the offense and the juvenile's amenability to treatment. If a person is tried as a juvenile, the police and court records are supposed to be confidential; however, as an adult, the young person carries a permanent police record.

Fine

Some offenses may result in the offender being ordered to pay a fine to the court and/or compensation to any victims who have suffered as a consequence of the offense. The court has the power to deduct the money from the offender's wages if necessary.

Sentencing

If found guilty of a more serious crime, the offender can be sentenced. The sentence depends on the nature of the offense and the person's past record. Serious and repeat offenders usually spend time in prison.

- **Probation:** The offender may receive a prison sentence but will not actually spend any time in prison. However, if found guilty of any further offenses during the probation period, the court will take this into consideration and will likely impose a more severe sentence as a consequence.

- **Youth Facility:** The 1991 Children in Custody Census found approximately 58,000 juveniles in various youth facilities. Currently, there are 1,076 facilities in which delinquents are incarcerated and rehabilitated. They include juvenile detention centers, training schools, juvenile halls, boys ranches, and group homes.

- Community Service. In this case, the offender, instead of being sent to prison, is ordered to work for a certain number of hours on a project that helps others. If the offender breaks the terms of the community service order, he/she will be returned to the courts for re-sentencing and may be sent to prison or a youth facility. Some offenders may be offered the chance to participate in a rehabilitation program as an alternative to going to prison. For example, drug addicts who have been found guilty of committing crimes are sometimes offered the opportunity to be treated for their addiction in a clinic.

Individual Activity

Hand out the following activity, and allow about ten minutes for students to complete the page.

ACTIVITY: What Makes a Criminal?

Personality and personal circumstances are often a major influences on whether or not a person commits criminal acts. Below is a list of personality traits. Put a check in the boxes of those traits that you think might help a person to live a happy, law-abiding life.

☐ Likes money, but doesn't like working for it

☐ Needs a lot of excitement in order to enjoy life

☐ Has lots of hobbies and interests

☐ Has a "macho-man" image and finds it difficult to behave in any other way

☐ Cares about people and does a lot of volunteer work in the community

☐ Has a goal in life and is determined to succeed

☐ Lacks will power and is easily led by others

☐ Has a chip on his/her shoulder and thinks society has treated him poorly

☐ Feels insecure and seeks attention

☐ Has an easy-going attitude and takes life as it comes

1. Consider those personality traits that you did not check. Use the space below to explain why those traits might lead people to commit criminal acts, and give examples of some of the crimes they might commit.

2. Explain why those traits you have checked might help a person to avoid trouble and live a happy, law-abiding life.

Small Group Case Study

Ask the class to form small groups, and hand out one copy of "Case Study: Eddie" per group. One member of each group should read the Background Information, then the group should discuss the questions that follow.

CASE STUDY: Eddie

Background Information

It was Vinnie who started it. He had an older brother who bragged he could disarm any car alarm system and hotwire the engine. Vinnie kept watch for his brother a couple of times while he stole some old junkers for a laugh. They never did any real harm. Trouble was, Vinnie had this thing about wanting to outdo his brother. He turned up at my place one night, loaded up with the tools his brother used for getting into cars.

Now, there was a guy who lived at the end of our street who gave us a lot of hassle. We called him Gooseneck because he was always sticking his big long neck out of his front door to see if any of us kids were messing around with his car. He had this new sporty hatchback that looked real flashy in our area, where most people couldn't even afford a new bicycle.

Vinnie said it would be a laugh to lift Gooseneck's car and drive it around. I wasn't sure about this, so I only agreed to keep watch while Vinnie showed what he could do. He fiddled around with the keys and bars for ages. There was no way he was going to get the lock open. Next thing I knew, he smashed the side window and dove into the driver's seat. The car alarm went off and all the lights in the neighborhood came on, but Vinnie just sat there revving the engine. Then Gooseneck opened his front door and Vinnie sped off, blowing the horn at him. I took off running, and he picked me up in the next street, and we drove around for a long time, doing spins and playing with all the car controls.

I was hooked after that. It was the biggest thrill I ever had, driving fast on country roads, slamming on the brakes, and getting the wheels off the ground as we spun around. We would drive a car until it was almost out of gas and then dump it. Or sometimes when we had finished with a car, we'd take it out in the middle of nowhere and torch it. That was fun, too. We felt powerful destroying something worth thousands of dollars. Doing that to someone else's property, it didn't feel so bad that we were poor and had nothing of our own.

CASE STUDY: Eddie (page 2)

We must have stolen twenty cars before the police caught up with us. I got away with probation the first time. It didn't stop me. It was like an addiction. I had to go out and get a car or else I'd just stay at home feeling miserable. But once the police get your name, they're at your house every time a car's missing. I ended up being sent to a youth facility, which was hard to take, but after that it was prison and that almost killed me.

I don't know where it would have ended if it hadn't been for Malcolm. He was my probation officer. I was looking at another prison sentence for the same old thing, stealing cars, but Malcolm made some deal to get me off if I promised to join this program he was running. It was supposed to be a kind of training for kids who couldn't keep their hands off other people's cars. There were seven of us and we used to meet at an old garage twice a week. Malcolm arranged for a mechanic to come along and teach us all about how cars work and how to service them. He also got hold of this old car for us to fix up. It was a total wreck, but when we started to do some work on it, we could really see it had potential. I was hooked again. I couldn't keep away from the garage and spent all my spare time working on that car. The other kids in the program were the same. The car looked really good once we had done some work on it—massive chrome plate bumpers, an engine that purred like a cat, leather upholstery and a polished walnut dashboard. I never thought I'd drive a car like that. I used to lie awake at night worrying in case someone stole it from the garage.

The day the car passed its smog test, Malcolm suggested we take it down to the stock car race at the local stadium. We weren't going to race it; we were just going to show it off in the car park. Malcolm said we ought to do something to celebrate, and he gave us all some money to go and buy hot dogs. When we came back, there he was holding this massive sledgehammer. The car? You couldn't recognize it. All the windows were smashed in, the bumpers ripped off and dented, the seats slashed. No one knew what to say at first; we were sick. Then some of the kids started to run up to Malcolm. I thought they were going to take him apart. They kept screaming at him, "Why did you do it? Why did you smash up our car?"

But I knew why.

CASE STUDY: Eddie (page 3)

Discussion Questions

Discuss the following questions, and write your answers in the space provided.

1. Suggest reasons why Vinnie was so determined to steal Gooseneck's sporty hatchback.

2. What did Eddie enjoy about stealing cars?

3. Choose two excerpts from the story that might explain why some young people steal cars.

4. Why do you think Malcolm smashed up the car? Do you think it will help the boys in any way? Why or why not?

5. Programs like the one Malcolm was running encourage some young car thieves to change their behavior for the better. What is it about these schemes—learning about car mechanics and repairing old cars—that has this effect?

Victims

Most crimes have a traumatic effect on the victims. Here are some examples from newspaper stories.

- Doctors say that an eighty-nine-year-old widow, Elsie Banks, is unlikely to regain the sight in one eye and has seriously impaired vision in the other after being attacked in her home by robbers.

- The parents of a seven-year-old girl told reporters how their daughter required extensive psychiatric treatment following an incident in which she found the family's pet cat hanging from a swing in an playground near her home. Two local youths were subsequently charged and convicted.

Even minor crimes like petty theft cause psychological stress and anxiety for innocent people. For example, a person who sees a handbag containing money in a cafe and decides to steal it doesn't know what the circumstances are of the person who owns the bag. The owner could be a mother on her own with four children who has just cashed a check for money to feed her family for the next couple of weeks.

Using the foregoing situation as a discussion starter, ask the group how they think the woman would feel upon discovering her purse missing.

Friends and relatives of criminals are also victims.

Ask the students to consider the following:

- How do you think your parents would react if you were accused or found guilty of an offense?

- How might they react if they received a late-night visit from the police informing them that you had been arrested?

- How do you think your friends would react if you were found guilty of an offense?

Small Group Case Study

Ask the class to form small groups, and hand out the following activity to each. Allow about ten to fifteen minutes for them to complete it.

ACTIVITY: Excuses, Excuses

People who commit crimes often make up excuses to justify their behavior. For example, a person who steals money from a handbag might say the owner should have taken better care of her property if she didn't want it stolen. This implies that it is the victim's fault that she had her money stolen.

Here is a list of crimes. In each case write down an excuse which the person committing the crime might give to justify his/her behavior.

- stabbing a person in a street fight
- stealing sweets from a supermarket
- sexually assaulting a friend
- stealing car stereos

Why do people who commit crimes make up these excuses? Discuss this and make a note of any conclusions you reach. Also discuss why people commit crimes even though their actions almost always involve hurting others.

Small Group Role-Play

Ask the class to form groups of three, and hand out one copy of the following role-play to each group. Each member should read one of the character parts, then the group should discuss the questions that follow.

After they have answered the questions, they should create their own role-plays to present to the class.

ROLE-PLAY: To Be an Accomplice

Here is a skit with three characters. Sharon and Linda are trying to persuade Jeanette to help them steal some CDs from a store. Choose a character and then read the skit in parts.

SHARON: Come on, Jeanette, we need your help.

JEANETTE: Can't you do it without me? I'll only mess it up.

LINDA: No way. There have to be three of us—one to keep the assistant busy, another to stand in front of the security camera so they don't get us on video, and the other to lift the tapes.

JEANETTE: You've got it all planned, haven't you?

SHARON: Yeah. Come on, Jeanette, it'll be totally easy with the three of us.

JEANETTE: My Dad would kill me if he found out.

LINDA: Are you scared?

JEANETTE: No.

SHARON: Jeanette, you can just stand in front of the camera if you want. You don't have to steal anything.

JEANETTE: Oh, I don't know.

LINDA: She's scared.

SHARON: Nothing will go wrong. It'll only take a couple of minutes.

JEANETTE: Can't you get someone else to do it?

ROLE-PLAY: To Be an Accomplice (page 2)

LINDA: I've had enough of this. If you don't come along, Jeanette, we're not going to let you hang around with us anymore.

JEANETTE: All right, then.

Discussion Questions

1. How did Linda and Sharon get Jeanette to do what they wanted?

2. Jeanette was trying to find reasons to get out of helping Sharon and Linda steal from the shop. Find two excerpts from the reading that illustrate this.

3. Instead of offering excuses, Jeanette might have said she wasn't interested in stealing the tapes and wouldn't change her mind under any circumstances. Why do some people find it difficult to be firm and say what they really think in situations like this?

Make up your own role-play. Sharon and Linda should still try to persuade Jeanette to steal from the shop, but this time Jeanette should be a more assertive person who gives clear reasons why she is not prepared to break the law and who actually tries to make Linda and Sharon see what risks they're taking.

4 *Drugs*

Before presenting this section, read over and decide which activities, role-plays, and / or case studies your class will do. Have photocopies of the selected pages ready to hand out.

The term "drugs" refers to chemical substances. Many chemical substances are used in medicine, under careful supervision, for treating the sick; others are too dangerous for people to use, even under medical care. However, these substances are still created or imported and used illegally. Illegal use of any drug is called "drug abuse."

People become "drug dependent" if they feel compelled to take a particular drug in order to experience its effect or to avoid the discomfort ("withdrawal") produced by its absence. This dependence can occur whether the drug is prescribed by a doctor, illegally sold on the streets, or legally sold over the counter (such as alcohol and nicotine).

- *Physical dependence* or *drug addiction* occurs when the body has become so accustomed to the drug that, on withdrawal from the drug, unpleasant physical symptoms arise.

- *Psychological dependence* or *drug habituation* occurs when someone thinks that he/she needs to continue taking a particular drug, even though no physical symptoms result on withdrawal from the drug.

For most drug users, a combination of both physical and psychological factors contributes to their dependence on a particular drug.

All drugs, even those used for medical treatment, can have potentially harmful side effects for the user. In theory, it is possible to become psychologically dependent on any drug. However, some drugs are more closely associated with the problem of dependency among users than others.

At this point in your presentation, have the class members spend about five minutes making a list of drugs they associate with the problem of drug dependency.

The media often stereotype "drug users" as people dependent on illegal substances such as cocaine and heroin. This is misleading; many people are dependent on other drugs, some of which are legal. For example, many people in the forty-five to sixty-four age group depend on barbiturates (Valium, Librium, Mogadon, etc.) prescribed by their doctors for treating medical problems such as sleeplessness and depression. Solvent abuse such as glue sniffing by young people can also cause dependency. Other substances widely associated with drug dependency include alcohol, nicotine, LSD or "acid," and the illegal barbiturates known as "downers" or "goofballs."

Cannabis (marijuana) has been linked with various medical disorders among users, and new research suggests that prolonged use of marijuana can lead to psychological dependence. Moreover, many people worry that using cannabis can be an introduction to more harmful drugs such as heroin.

Some medicinal uses of marijuana, such as the treatment of glaucoma and the nausea associated with chemotherapy, have caused much national debate about its legalization.

Small Group Activity

Ask the class to form small groups. Hand out one activity page per group, and give them about five minutes to complete the first part.

When the small groups are done, compile a whole-group list from their lists. Ask the small groups to select the three least-convincing (in their opinions) reasons for smoking pot and explain their choices to the whole group.

ACTIVITY: Why Smoke Pot?

Spend five minutes making a list of reasons why someone at your school might smoke pot:

After the whole-group list is compiled, write the three least-convincing reasons (in your opinion) to smoke pot below. Be prepared to explain your choices.

Who Is Using Drugs?

Not surprisingly, juvenile delinquents are using drugs. The more serious a youth's involvement in delinquency, the more serious the youth's involvement in drug use, and vice versa. This applies to all age, gender, and ethnic groups.

However, drug and alcohol abuse is a major problem for many more young people who are not involved in delinquency. There are an estimated three million adolescent alcoholics in this country. Many high school students see alcohol as the "drug of choice," and, as a result, alcohol abuse is the most widespread drug abuse problem. No reliable data exist for the number of youth addicted to illegal drugs, but the juvenile arrest rates for heroin/cocaine increased dramatically between 1980 and 1990—more than seven hundred percent.

Drug dependence is a process. After initial use or "experimentation," a person may continue "casual" or "recreational" use. If dependence results, drug use will become more regular and may be accompanied by "tolerance," when the body changes under the influence of the drug so that more of the drug is required to produce the same effect. Finally, a person may temporarily succeed in quitting the drug but start using it (or another) again after a period of abstinence.

Small Group Activity

Ask the class to form small groups. Hand out one activity page per group. Allow about ten minutes, then discuss their answers in the whole group.

ACTIVITY: Drug Abuse and Its Consequences

Discuss the following, then write your answers in the space provided. Be prepared to discuss your answers in the whole group.

1. Assume that a heroin addict has a $100-per-day habit. Suggest three ways in which he/she might get the money to buy the drug.

2. Make a list of symptoms which you think might be associated with withdrawal from drugs.

3. "Drugs can ruin your life." Give five examples of how drugs can have this effect.

Types of Drugs

Heroin

Heroin is a synthetic drug with many street names, including "H," "Harry," and "smack." It is usually sold in the form of a white powder. Addicts are known as "junkies." Death from overdosing is not common; death is more likely to occur from the injection of much purer heroin than the user is used to. Death can also occur by suffocating on one's own vomit because people often vomit the first few times they try heroin. Sharing needles can spread serum hepatitis and HIV, among other infections. Withdrawal can cause severe pains, anxiety, and nausea. The term "cold turkey" refers to the chills accompanied by goose pimples one experiences during withdrawal.

Cocaine

Cocaine, also known as "coke," "snow," or "C," is usually sold as a white, bitter-tasting crystalline powder. Usually, it is sniffed—"snorted"—but it may also be injected or smoked. Its use in the United States is currently increasing, and, to some extent, it still has the reputation of being a glamorous drug. With regular use, the user may become restless, sleepless, feel sick, and lose weight. However, the main danger from cocaine arises from the extreme physical and psychological dependency it can induce.

Crack is a form of cocaine which is smoked. Some authorities claim that one use is enough to cause addiction. For the user to gain the maximum effect, crack may have to be taken as often as once an hour. This is a very expensive habit. Crack has been responsible for thousands of deaths among young people in America and it is feared that this trend will spread to other countries.

LSD

LSD and other drugs which change the way you perceive your surroundings are known as *hallucinogens*. Overdosing is a real danger with hallucinogens, especially phencyclidine and "Angel Dust" or PCP. Some people on "bad trips" commit suicide; others die as a result of the drug-induce irrational sense of power that causes them to attempt impossible feats such as flying from high buildings or stopping oncoming cars by will power.

Ecstasy

Ecstasy is a drug which combines both stimulant and hallucinogenic effects but allows the person to stay more in control than LSD. Ecstasy is a popular drug on the youth drug scene as it allows users to dance for longer periods. It is an exceptionally poisonous drug: the dose necessary for an effect is sufficient to destroy brain cells. Death can occur through overheating and dehydration.

Solvents

Solvents include a wide range of compounds—not just glue—that either emit fumes or are gases. Inhalation tends to depress bodily functions such as breathing and heart rate. The effects are often compared to being drunk or in a dream. Long-term abuse of solvents can lead to liver and kidney damage, and deaths have resulted from choking on one's own vomit.

Alcohol

The more alcohol a person drinks, the more difficult he/she generally finds it to stop drinking. The common withdrawal symptoms are:

- increased irritability
- shakiness
- insomnia
- sweating
- nausea

Long-term alcohol consumption in large amounts may lead to progressive damage to the brain, the liver, and the stomach, among other health problems.

Hand out the following activity page to each student, and allow about ten minutes to complete it.

Individual Activity

ACTIVITY: Finding Alternatives to Drugs

Below is a list of reasons people give for taking drugs. In each case, suggest safer ways of achieving the same effect. For example, if the reason for taking drugs is to relax, a safer alternative might be to read a book, listen to music, or join a yoga class.

Reason for taking drugs   **Safer alternatives**

To lose weight

To feel more energetic

To rebel

To relieve anxiety

To relieve boredom

To build up the body

To aid sleep

To impress others

To help late-night study

To avoid feeling sad

The Law and Drugs

Consider researching the drug laws in your state to supplement the following discussion.

Although drug laws differ from state to state, the following are general guidelines governing drug use:

- It is illegal for anyone under twenty-one to buy alcohol.
- It is illegal to possess, use, buy, or sell "controlled substances" such as marijuana, cocaine, heroin, etc.
- It is illegal to drive under the influence of alcohol or any other drug.

To help enforce the law, police can search a vehicle in the following circumstances:

- if the situation is an emergency
- if the person driving gives consent
- if they have a warrant
- if they have reasonable cause to believe illegal drugs are in the vehicle
- if the owner has been arrested or is in custody for some other offense
- if they capture the vehicle driver after "hot pursuit"
- if the driver is on parole or probation

With a search warrant, the police may also enter premises to search for illegal drugs.

Small Group Activity

Ask the class to form small groups. Hand out one activity page to each group, then allow about ten minutes to complete it. After the small groups are done, compile a whole group list, then ask the small groups to select the three greatest risks (in their opinion) of abusing drugs.

ACTIVITY: Reasons to "Just Say No"

Make a list of reasons why a drug user might eventually regret getting involved with drugs.

After the whole class list is compiled, write the three greatest risks involved with taking drugs below. Be prepared to explain your choices.

Who Can Help?

There are no simple solutions for helping people who abuse drugs. It is always easier to start taking drugs than to stop; however, a person who has a drug dependency problem and wants to stop taking the drugs will find that help is available from various sources:

- People often consult their doctors first after realizing they have a problem. Doctors can offer advice and refer patients to special agencies for dealing with drug problems.

- Drug rehabilitation centers exist specifically to provide professional help to those with an acknowledged drug problem.

- Therapeutic communities and residential units provide an environment in which, through discussion and group work, addicts help themselves and each other to overcome problems.

- Informal drug advisory centers offer advice to anyone needing more information about drugs.

- Recovery groups such as Alcoholics Anonymous and Narcotics Anonymous are led by people in recovery who have first-hand experience of drug problems and, as such, gain the trust and confidence of other group members.

- Counselors often work voluntarily for helping agencies. Such people can talk through problems with a person and help him/her identify alternative courses of action.

- Schools provide education about drugs. Staff and faculty may identify pupils with a problem and support them while they get help.

- Family and friends provide the encouragement, support, and love necessary to help the drug abuser deal with the problem and to resist any temptation to start taking drugs again in the future.

Small Group Role-Play

Ask the class to form groups of three. Hand out one role-play sheet per group. The students will enact their role-plays in their small groups only. After five or ten minutes, ask each small group to report to the whole group the arguments each character used. Ask those who played Debbie how easy or difficult it was to resist accepting the pills.

ROLE-PLAY: Will she or won't she?

Background Information

Debbie feels depressed because she just received her algebra exam results, which were not very good. She goes to a party at a friend's house and meets Phil, who offers her some pills which he says will cheer her up. Helen, a friend of Debbie's, sees what is happening and comes over to persuade Debbie not to take the drugs.

Three-Minute Role-Play

Decide who will enact the parts of Debbie, Phil, and Helen. Base your role-play on what might happen as Helen and Phil try to convince Debbie one way or the other.

5 Gangs

Before presenting this section, read over and decide which activities, role-plays, and/or case studies your class will do. Have photocopies of the selected pages ready to hand out.

When the word "gang" is used today, chances are it doesn't conjure up the image of a band of old school chums, as it did in earlier generations. Today, the word "gang" is associated with groups of youth who violate the law. Gang members range in age from twelve to twenty-five, with seventeen being the peak age. Few female gangs exist.

Gangs are committing more violent crimes, inflicting more serious injuries, and using more lethal weapons than ever before. The FBI reports that the Crips and Bloods of Los Angeles have migrated to as many as forty-five western and midwestern cities.

Individual Activity

Ask if any class members belong to a gang. (Be prepared for what you may hear.) Explain that most students belong to "gangs" in the sense that they have groups they hang around with.

Hand out the activity page to each student. Allow five to ten minutes to complete it.

Optional: Lead a discussion about gang activity in your school or community, with the understanding that anything shared in the classroom will be kept confidential.

ACTIVITY: Gangs As You See Them

Describe how you think a gang is organized. If you have no idea, imagine what one is like. Does it have a name? Where does it meet? How many members does it have? Who is the leader? What does the gang do together? For example, do they provide a community service? Do they ever get into trouble and/or break the law?

Teenage Gangs

Most gangs, especially those consisting mainly of teens, have certain things in common.

- The gang usually has a name or a symbol that identifies the group. One notorious street gang in New York was known as the Cobras; members had a tattoo of a snake on their right forearms.

- The members of the gang have their own style, which may be expressed in the clothes they wear, the way they behave in public, and the language they use.

- The gang has activities which are central to its identity; for example, cruising may be the main activity for some gangs.

- Often, a gang follows certain rituals in its activities; that is, the same activities are carried out in the same way at specified times. For example, a gang of football fans may meet every Sunday morning at the local park for a pickup game followed by a couple of hours of drinking in a local bar.

- Members identify strongly with the gang and may see it as one of the most important things in their lives.

- Gangs are often hard to join; prospective members may have to prove themselves by taking part in an initiation ceremony. For example, to join the Cobras, a person had to jump from the roof of one high-rise building to another across a gap of about eight feet.

- Gangs, especially those which get into trouble, usually have rival gangs who have a different style or set of values.

Small Group Activity

Ask the class to form small groups. Hand out the activity page, and allow about ten minutes to complete it. Invite each small group to share its findings with the whole class. Again, stress that anything shared in this discussion will be kept confidential.

ACTIVITY: Gang Identities

Next to each of the following common features of a gang, write at least one example from a gang you know. If you don't personally know a gang, imagine what some of these features might be.

- name and/or symbol

- style of clothing,
  behavior, or language

- activities

- rituals

- strong member identification

- initiation ceremonies

- rival gangs

Street Smarts © 1995 Resource Publications, Inc.

How Some Gangs Get into Trouble

Some reasons follow which might explain why gangs get into trouble even though they don't always intend to.

- Individual gang members may behave badly because they think that this is the way other members of the gang expect them to behave. For example, members of a gang of football fans may taunt and jeer the supporters of an opposing team because they believe that this is the way to show their loyalty and commitment to the gang. As individuals, they may not want to behave in this way and might be worried about the trouble they could cause; however, they may not stop acting in this way for fear of looking weak and losing face with the other gang members.

- Tension between rival gangs can spark trouble when they come into contact with each other. Some gangs may go out looking to start fights with other gangs, but, more often, when two or more gangs clash, their paths have crossed accidentally.

- Sometimes gangs behave badly as a reaction to the way they are treated by other people. For example, some older people may have a negative, hostile attitude toward gangs, perhaps feeling afraid or seeing them as a challenge to their own values.

- Some gang leaders may want to prove that they are tough by causing trouble. These people may not be brave enough to act alone, so they try to get the gang involved. If other members of the gang are not strong enough to resist, they may find themselves getting into fights and breaking the law even though they are not really troublemakers.

Individual Activity

Ask the class to write a short essay (about five hundred words) explaining how a gang might get into trouble even though the individual members may not want this to happen.

Small Group Case Study

Ask the class to form small groups. Hand out the following case study to each group. Allow about thirty minutes for them to read the case study and answer the questions that follow. Then invite the small group to share their answers with the whole group.

CASE STUDY: Vince

Background Information

In the beginning, we were just a group of guys who hung out together. We would get a little loud sometimes, but we never got into any serious trouble. There was a field where we used to meet and play football or ride motorcycles. But then the land was sold and they built a warehouse on the site. We still met there because we didn't have anywhere else to go, but it wasn't the same. We tried to play football at night in the parking lot of the warehouse, but the owners found out and put up a big fence to keep us out. To get back at them, we would climb the fence and let the air out of the tires of the delivery trucks parked outside the warehouse at night.

One time we noticed that the door at the back of one of the trucks was unlocked and there were bags of chips inside. We formed a line and passed the boxes along until we emptied the truck.

We ate as many chips as we could that night, then dumped the rest. It was just a case of getting back at the warehouse people for kicking us out. Anyway, it was fun. I guess we were bored, too, because there was nothing else to do.

We left the warehouse alone for a few weeks after that, but then we got the idea of stealing from the trucks again. Everyone dared each other to climb the fence first. Finally, everyone piled over and one of my friends used a metal bar to smash his way into a truck. He hotwired the engine and began to drive around. No one expected him to do that. When he crashed the truck into the front window of the warehouse, most of us got scared and ran off. A couple of guys went inside the warehouse through the broken window and stole some candy and drinks. The police showed up, and eventually we all ended up in court.

With trespassing, stealing, and breaking and entering on my record, it was difficult to get a job when I left school. So, to get money, eight of us from the original gang started stealing car radios. We started drinking and making a nuisance of ourselves. One night a group of older guys who considered this one bar their territory challenged us in the parking lot after closing time. They beat the daylights out of Danny, our leader.

CASE STUDY: Vince (page 2)

Danny quit the gang after that and Albert started to push his way to the front. No one really liked Albert. He was vicious and always wanted to prove himself. I suppose he couldn't help how he was. I know his dad used to knock him around a lot at home when he was a kid. But Danny would never have done half the things Albert got us to do. We should have stood up to him and stopped him, but we were too weak or too stupid.

Albert kept going on about how we had been pushed out of the bar and what we should do about it. He got us worked up one night and we went down to the bar. They didn't have a chance. Albert had a switchblade and the rest of us had metal pipes. But then one of the guys Albert was fighting with got his switchblade off him. Albert panicked and pulled a gun. None of us knew he had brought a gun along. I just saw the guy go down. He died later in hospital.

Albert was charged with murder, and, at first, so were the rest of us. The police assumed we were all responsible for the death because we had all gone to the bar intending to start a fight. Later, our charges were dropped to manslaughter. Albert was found guilty of murder and got twenty years in prison. The rest of us got three years each.

Discussion Questions

The gang in the story started out as a group of friends who hung around together. They weren't troublemakers at first, but later they became involved in criminal activities. Answer the following questions, then be prepared to share your answers with the whole group.

1. Things began to go wrong for the gang when they lost the field where they used to meet. Make a list of the other main events that led up to the gang becoming involved in serious criminal activities.

CASE STUDY: Vince (page 3)

2. Choose two excerpts that suggest that Vince was not really a troublemaker and didn't want to break the law.

3. Suggest reasons which might explain why the gang allowed Albert to take over without any resistance.

4. Without actually leaving the gang, what could Vince have done to (a) stop himself from getting into trouble and (b) stop the rest of the gang from getting into trouble?

5. Give two reasons why a person might stay in a gang that is breaking the law even though he/she doesn't want to get into trouble.

Whole Group Activity

Invite the class to discuss either or both of the following statements:

- Girls don't join gangs, or if they do, they don't get into trouble.
- Teenagers today are not interested in joining gangs.

Small Group Activity

Ask the class to form two groups. Hand out the role-play on the following page. Allow about ten minutes for them to read the background information and create their role-play.

After the groups have presented their role-plays, lead a discussion about what could be done to help the bikers and the residents get along better.

ROLE-PLAY: Leather Gang Invades Sunny Park

Background Information

Sunny Park is a neighborhood of apartments occupied mainly by middle-aged people and senior citizens. The residents are fed up with a gang of bikers who ride up and down the street, blowing their horns throughout the evening and often late at night. The bikers wear leather and do a lot of swearing and shouting. Some of the people living in Sunny Park find the gang intimidating. However, the members of the gang don't see themselves as troublemakers.

Five-Minute Role-Play

Divide your group in half: bikers and Sunny Park residents. Create a role-play of a confrontation that occurs when some residents go out to tell the bikers that they are a nuisance and are not wanted in the area. Try to imagine how each side feels and what they might say to each other.

Small Group Activity

Ask the class to form small groups. Hand out the activity page and allow about ten minutes for them to complete it. Then invite the groups to share their proposals with the large group. Can the class approach the community with their ideas?

ACTIVITY: Keep Kids off the Street

Imagine that you are community-relations officers in an area where there is not much for young people to do with their time. Discuss what your community might do to provide more entertainment and leisure activities for the young people in the area. Use the space below to write down your three best proposals.

6 Sexual Exploitation

Before presenting this section, read over and decide which activities, role-plays, and/or case studies your class will do. Have photocopies of the selected pages ready to hand out.

Sexual exploitation refers to any situation in which an individual (or group) takes advantage of another person to manipulate and control his/her sexual behavior. Sexual exploitation can take many forms. One example is the person popularly known as a pimp, who makes a profit by controlling and regulating the activity of a prostitute.

Pornography is another form of sexual exploitation. While some of the models/actors may freely choose to take part, others do so only because they are pressured into it. It could also be argued that the people who buy pornography are being exploited. Their need for sexual satisfaction is being manipulated by the producers of pornography in order to make a profit.

Some consider seduction to be a subtle form of sexual exploitation. One person seduces another by using sexual attraction to undermine the other person's will to resist. The problem is whether subtle persuasion, rather than actual domination or manipulation, is taking place; whether or not the seduction involves sexual exploitation depends on the context in which it occurs.

Individual Activity

Hand out the activity sheet on the following page to each student. Allow about fifteen or twenty minutes to complete it, then discuss the questions in the large group.

ACTIVITY: The Question of Sexual Exploitation

Read the following four stories, then answer the questions on the next page.

Dan has been going out with Jill for three months. He wants to go to bed with her, but she isn't ready yet. Dan knows Jill likes him, and he decides to use this to his advantage. He threatens to drop Jill if she doesn't agree to sleep with him.

Dawn is fifteen. Every Saturday night she babysits for her older sister who lives on the other side of town. Afterward, her sister's husband gives her a lift home. But recently he has started coming on to her, taking detours and parking the car on dark side streets. He refuses to take Dawn home unless she kisses him first. He knows he can get away with it because Dawn wouldn't want to say anything to upset her sister's marriage.

Julie has been going out with Chris for nearly a year. Chris is so shy he has to turn the lights off just to give Julie a kiss. Julie likes Chris, but she wants a bit more action and knows she will have to make the first move. One night she invites Chris to her place, puts on a sexy dress, turns the lights down, and spikes his soda without him knowing. Once the alcohol has taken effect on Chris, she sets about seducing him.

John and Barry are supposed to be friends, but secretly John can't stand Barry. He is big and brash and everything John isn't. Barry has a fiancée, Shelley, but their relationship has been rough recently. John sees this as an opportunity to put one over on Barry and starts to use his charm to win Shelley's affection. He comforts her after she has had arguments with Barry; when Barry humiliates her in public, John takes her side and pays her compliments. John can't believe what a slimebag he is being, but it seems to be working because the other day he noticed Shelley looking at him affectionately. When they were alone, he kissed her softly and she didn't stop him.

ACTIVITY: The Question of Sexual Exploitation (page 2)

Questions

1. Which, if any, of the previous stories are examples of sexual exploitation? (Recall the definition of sexual exploitation as "any situation in which an individual takes advantage of another to manipulate and control his/her sexual behavior.") Give reasons for your answers.

2. Why do some people allow themselves to be exploited sexually? Make a list of points and illustrate your answer by referring to the stories above and any examples which you know about from your own experience.

3. Give two examples of how a person might suffer serious emotional or physical harm as a consequence of being exploited sexually.

4. Answer yes or no to the following and give reasons why or why not.
   • Should Jill go to bed with Dan?

   • Should Dawn tell her sister what her husband is up to?

   • Should Chris be mad at Julie for what she has done?

   • Should Shelley tell Barry what's happening between her and John?

Why Does It Happen?

Sexual exploitation happens for a number of reasons. With some forms of sexual exploitation, the main goal is financial profit. Pornography, for example, is a multi-million-dollar business.

The motive with other forms of sexual exploitation may be more personal; for example, the exploiter might be seeking to satisfy his/her own selfish sexual needs, or he/she might have a perverse desire to abuse and humiliate the other person or to act out fantasies of power and control.

Sexual exploitation is a way for some people to release their feelings of emotional and/or sexual frustration (though this in no way justifies the exploitation or makes it acceptable). Some men exploit their female partners as a way of asserting their power within the relationship.

People are subjected to sexual exploitation in ways that vary from physical force or mental cruelty at one extreme (as in rape and some forms of sexual abuse within marriage) to subtle forms of manipulation at the other (seduction, erotic imagery, advertising techniques). In many cases, a mixture of punishments and rewards is used by the exploiter to get his/her own way. Sometimes, the sheer dependence and vulnerability of the other person make the process of exploitation easy. This is particularly the case with sexual abuse of young children within the family.

Individual Activity

Hand out the following activity page to each student and allow about fifteen minutes to complete it. Then invite them to share their answers in the large group.

ACTIVITY: Advice Column

Imagine that you are the editor of an advice column in a magazine for young people. You have received two requests for advice from people who are being sexually exploited (the details are given below). Write a short reply to each, making practical suggestions about what the person should do.

Duncan is 19 and very ambitious. He works as a trainee accountant in a big company and is aiming for the top. He has a problem with his new boss, though. Even though she is married, she has made it clear that she likes him and would like to have an affair with him. He has tried to avoid her and ignore her suggestions, but he is scared to tell her straight out that he is not interested in case she gets angry and decides to sabotage his chances of promotion in the company. Things are getting worse; the other day she arranged for him to work as her personal assistant and told him that he could go a long way in his career with her help. Duncan is sure it is all going to end in disaster. What should he do?

Pauline is a quiet girl who gets bullied a lot by the other girls at her boarding school. Much of the responsibility for discipline at the school is left in the hands of the older students. Two of the older students have started to pick on Pauline and have forced her to run errands for them and act as their personal servant. They are also sexually abusing her. When she threatened to complain, one of them twisted her arm behind her back and the other pulled her hair. They said that this was just a taste of what she would get if she complained. Should Pauline complain? How would you reassure her that everything will be all right?

Prostitution

Though it may seem that prostitutes have chosen their way of life in preference to other ways of living, the reality is usually more complex.

Many female prostitutes are unmarried mothers struggling to support young children alone. Others are drug addicts who use their earnings from prostitution to support their habit.

Alternative ways of earning a living may not be available to these women due to a high level of unemployment in their community or because they lack qualifications and proven work skills. They could survive on welfare, but some women turn to prostitution anyway in order to pay off debts or get extra money to buy presents for their children. Once they start to earn money in this way, it may be difficult to stop.

Many prostitutes come from backgrounds in which they were sexually abused, sometimes from an early age. As a consequence, they may have low self-esteem which makes them vulnerable to being exploited as prostitutes.

Some prostitutes argue that if they hadn't turned to prostitution, their lives would be even more degrading. For example, they may have turned to prostitution in order to escape husbands, boyfriends, or fathers who beat them up.

Prostitutes are often exploited by pimps, who live off their earnings. It could be argued that they are also exploited by their clients. Offering money for sex may in itself be a form of exploitation, given the impoverished position of the typical prostitute, but there are other more blatant ways in which clients take advantage of prostitutes. Examples include offering extra money to have oral sex or sexual intercourse without using a condom (not using a condom significantly increases the risk of contracting HIV and other sexually transmitted diseases) and having sex with a prostitute and then refusing to pay.

Some young men and women who are homeless are enticed into having sex in exchange for shelter, money, or food. This is a clear example of sexual exploitation with the underlying cause being poverty and social deprivation.

Individual Case Study

Hand out the case study to each student, and allow about ten minutes to complete it. Then invite the class to share their thoughts.

CASE STUDY: Judith

Background Information

At seventeen, Judith was still at school, retaking her SATs. Her ambition was to train to become a veterinary nurse. She came from a good home with loving parents, and, though she was a sensitive person, she seemed happy and relaxed. She had a steady boyfriend, and they planned to get married in a couple of years when they had saved some money.

At nineteen, Judith was unemployed and living alone in a run-down apartment in another town. She had no real friends, had lost contact with her parents, and had turned to prostitution.

Short Essay

Use the space below to explain what might have happened to Judith to bring about such a change in her life.

Circumstances of Sexual Exploitation

Sexual exploitation can exist in any relationship between two or more people. However, it is more likely to occur in some social contexts than in others:

- Poverty and Economic Hardship. People who are poor or who desperately need money for whatever reason are more vulnerable to sexual exploitation than others. Single unmarried mothers may turn to prostitution because they see it as the only effective means of supporting their children; likewise, young actors struggling to become established in their chosen career may, out of financial necessity, agree to perform in pornographic films.

- Economic Dependence. Children's dependence on adults makes them particularly vulnerable to sexual abuse. In some situations, parents may allow their children to become prostitutes because they can find no other means of supporting the family. Additionally, women may submit to sexual abuse from their partners upon whom they are financially dependent.

- Authority. Unscrupulous people who have power and authority can use their position as a means of exploiting others for sexual purposes. For example, an employer might persuade an employee to tolerate sexual advances by threatening dismissal if he/she refuses. Likewise, adults who sexually abuse children abuse their authority by threatening the children not to tell.

- Physical Power. In some relationships, men may use their strength to overpower women as a means of sexual exploitation. Women may be forced to engage in sexual acts which they find degrading by male partners who threaten physical violence.

- Lack of Education. Lack of knowledge may make a person vulnerable to sexual exploitation. Parents and other caring adults must teach children what unacceptable behavior might be and reinforce their belief that they will be safe if they need to talk about an incident.

- Closed Institutions. Sexual exploitation occurs in prisons, children's homes, mental institutions, and elder care homes, where occupants who attract sexual attention have few means of protecting themselves. The authorities often find it impossible to provide adequate supervision at all times, and many reports from prisoners and those in other institutions claim that other inmates or caregivers pressured or forced them into participating in sexual practices.

Whole Group Activity

Divide the class in half. Assign one of the following statements to each half. Each group will spend about fifteen minutes formulating arguments for their statement. After time is up, the two sides will debate why sexual exploitation occurs. The first speaker speaks for thirty seconds, then the speaker from the opposite group speaks for thirty seconds, then alternate back and forth until all members have presented an argument.

- Sexual exploitation occurs only because some people are too weak to resist the demands of others. If they had more will power, they would not be exploited.

- Sometimes people find themselves in situations in which it is difficult—even impossible—to stop other people from taking advantage of them sexually.

Whole Group Activity

Hand out the activity page to each student, and allow about ten minutes to complete it. Then invite students to share their answers with the whole group.

ACTIVITY: Homeless and Vulnerable

"A few nights sleeping under cardboard boxes makes the offer of a warm bed irresistible, whoever makes the offer and whatever strings are attached"
— a homeless teenager

Apart from not having anywhere to stay, what else might make a homeless young person vulnerable to sexual exploitation?

Answer this question by writing either a short essay or short story below (continue on the back if you need more space):

Street Violence

Before presenting this section, read over and decide which activities, role-plays, and/or case studies your class will do. Have photocopies of the selected pages ready to hand out.

Juveniles are involved in nearly one in five violent crimes occurring on the streets. According to the FBI, violent crimes include murder, rape, robbery, and aggravated assault.

Ask the students to think about why young people become involved in street violence. They may write their reasons on paper if they wish.

Why Does Street Violence Happen?

Present the following points to the class as reasons why young people are more likely than other age groups to be involved in violent incidents.

1. They visit the places where violence tends to occur, e.g., parties, bars/dance clubs, etc.

2. They are out late at night when a lot of physical assaults take place.

3. They often lack the material means to protect themselves and avoid trouble; for example, a teenager may have to walk home alone late at night

because he/she does not have a car or cannot afford to ride the bus.

4. Some young people lack the experience to avoid danger or to know how to handle situations without getting into a fight or provoking violence.

5. Young people have fewer responsibilities, so they have less incentive to avoid trouble.

6. Young people have less control over their emotions and are generally more volatile than older people.

7. Young people get involved with gangs and this can lead them into trouble.

Ask the students if they agree with these points. In particular, do they agree with numbers 5 and 6? Now invite them to share any further reasons they thought of earlier.

Individual Activity

Hand out the activity page to each student and allow about ten minutes to complete it. They should keep their papers for the next section, which covers the places, circumstances, and consequences associated with street violence.

ACTIVITY: Street Violence—Where, Why, & Then What?

Try to imagine three situations in which a young person might become involved in a violent incident in a public place. In each case, you should briefly describe:

- the place where the violence occurs
- the circumstances that led up to the violence
- the consequences for the young person

Write your three situations below:

1.

2.

3.

Place, Circumstances, & Consequences of Street Violence

Place

Violent acts can occur anywhere, but some places are more likely than others:

- places where gangs meet, such as parks, etc.
- parties
- sporting events
- busy shopping areas
- political demonstrations
- rock concerts
- bars/dance clubs, especially at closing time
- vacation resorts where young people are staying

Circumstances

The circumstances that can lead people to behave violently on the street include:

- Drugs, including alcohol. These can remove inhibitions and can make people bad-tempered and aggressive. People who have drug dependency problems may commit violent acts in desperation if they cannot obtain the drugs they require.
- Sex. A lot of fights start as quarrels between two people who are rivals for the affections of a third person.
- Gangs. Some gangs look for trouble; others attract it because they have a distinctive style of dress or way of life that other gangs don't like.
- Prejudice. Hate crimes motivated by fear of people of different race or sexual orientation occur regularly.
- Pride. Many fights occur between people who have been in conflict and cannot bring themselves to let down their defenses to reconcile their differences.

Consequences

The consequences for any young person who becomes involved in street violence, whether or not he/she provoked the incident, include:

- confrontation with the police, which could lead to a criminal record or even time in a detention center or prison

- loss of friends who don't like being associated with someone who attracts trouble

- arguments at home, especially if parents think that their child could have avoided the trouble

- loss of job

- long-term physical injuries, psychological problems, and, in some cases, loss of life

Small Group Activity

Ask the class to form small groups. Hand out the activity page and allow about fifteen to twenty minutes to complete it.

ACTIVITY: "I Like Fighting"

Some people say they like fighting and aren't really bothered about the consequences for themselves or others. Consider the following questions and write your answers in the spaces provided.

1. Do people who say they like fighting really mean it?

2. What might people like about fighting?

3. If people like fighting, should they be allowed to just go at it? What could be done to stop them? Make a list of suggestions.

4. Are people who choose to get involved in fights selfish? If so, what is selfish about it?

**Small Group
Activity**

Ask the class to form small groups, then hand out one case study page per group. Allow about thirty minutes for them to complete it.

CASE STUDY: Pete

Background Information

Pete and Dave used to be good friends, but they stopped hanging around together after Dave accused Pete of taking his girlfriend, Linda, from him. A few months later, they were all at the same party. Pete was with Linda and a friend, Joe. Dave was with a group of friends, including Phil, nicknamed "Tonka" because he was built like a truck and wasn't afraid of trouble. Dave's friends taunted him, suggesting he ought to go over and have it out with Pete about taking his girl. But Dave didn't want any trouble. Then Tonka stepped in and said he would sort it out. Pete was drinking beer from a can, so Tonka went over and pretended to bump into him. The beer spilled on Pete's clothes, and some went on Linda, too. Tonka told Pete to watch where he was going and added that he was too young to be drinking beer.

Pete knew Tonka was trying to provoke him, so he decided to ignore what happened. But Linda got all fired up and gave Tonka a piece of her mind. Tonka started to swear at Linda and call her names. Joe pulled Pete to one side and said, "He spilled your beer and now he's putting down your girl. If you don't say anything, they'll think you're a coward."

Pete was angry and confused now. The fact that he had been drinking didn't help. He grabbed hold of Tonka and told him to lay off Linda. Next thing you know, they were fighting. Dave tried to get between them to stop the fight, but Joe thought Dave was joining in on Tonka's side, so he stepped in to help Pete. All four were still fighting when the police arrived.

They were arrested and spent the night in custody. Eventually, the police released them with a warning. Tonka had sprained his wrist in the fight and was unable to work for six weeks. When he returned to work, the boss told him that he had given the job to someone else.

Discussion Questions

1. Whom do you blame for starting the fight? Why?

CASE STUDY: Pete (page 2)

2. Pete didn't really want to get into a fight with Tonka, so why did he?

3. As Pete's friends, what could Linda and Joe have done to prevent the fight?

4. How would you describe Dave's behavior during the incident?

5. Was Joe right to join in the fight on Pete's side?

6. Pete received a warning from the police. That means if he gets in trouble again, the police will probably prosecute him and he could end up in a youth facility. Imagine that you are Pete's parents. What advice would you give him about how to avoid getting involved in any more fights?

How to Avoid Trouble

- Stay clear of places where fights are likely to start.
- Be aware that drugs, including alcohol, can make you more aggressive.
- Don't walk home late at night, especially if you are alone.
- Don't go looking for trouble alone or in a group.
- Discourage the people you are with from getting into fights.
- If another person comes looking for trouble, stay calm and walk away.
- If you have been threatened with violence or think that you might be attacked, seek advice from older people and involve the police if necessary.

Invite the students to add more points to this list.

Small Group Activity

Ask the class to form small groups. Hand out the activity page and allow about fifteen to twenty minutes for them to complete it. Then invite the small groups to share their answers with the large group, giving reasons why they agree or disagree.

ACTIVITY: Agree or Disagree?

Read the following statements, then answer the questions. Be prepared to support your answers in a class discussion.

1. "Today, it is a good idea for young people to learn self-defense." Do you agree? Why or why not? Under what circumstances would a person be justified in using self-defense skills against another person?

2. "In a fight in the boxing ring, someone is declared a winner. In a street fight, there are no winners—just losers." Is this true? Support your answer.

3. "Some people are violent by nature and there is not much you can do to change them." Do you agree? Why or why not?

Small Group Role-Play

Ask the class to form groups of five. Hand out the role-play to each group and allow about ten minutes for them to create both versions. Decide if you want each group to present one or both of their role-plays.

ROLE-PLAY: Violence in the Workplace

Background Information

Bev, Diane, and Clare work in the same automotive factory. Recently, two new trainees, Wendy and Sonia, joined the production line. This caused some problems for Bev, Diane, and Clare because Wendy and Sonia stick together and don't socialize with them. Also, the two trainees work harder than the others and get a lot of praise from the managers.

Bev, Diane, and Clare want to stop Wendy and Sonia from working so hard and making them look bad with the managers. They decide to have it out with Wendy and Sonia one afternoon in the breakroom.

Three-Minute Role-Play

Decide who will play the roles of these five characters. Pick up the scene as they meet in the breakroom. Each character should be aggressive and not back down, calling each other names and maybe pushing and shoving. Your goal is to show how the argument between the girls could easily erupt into a fight.

Then create a second role-play. This time Wendy and Sonia should stay calm and refuse to be drawn into an argument or a fight even though Bev, Diane, and Clare behave aggressively toward them. Your goal is to show how Wendy and Sonia can avoid trouble by not allowing themselves to be provoked.

8 *Homelessness*

Before presenting this section, read over and decide which activities, role-plays, and/or case studies your class will do. Have photocopies of the selected pages ready to hand out.

Homelessness is a disturbing fact of life in American cities today. It is difficult to get an exact count of the homeless; the Census Bureau only count people in households. Homeless people often avoid officials because they are afraid they will be arrested or that their children will be taken from them. The best numbers available estimate the homeless population at between 300,000 and 400,000 people.

Of this very fluid homeless population, a large number are young people—either runaways or "throwaways." For example, of the 450,700 children and adolescents who ran away in 1990, 133,500 were without a place to stay at least one night when they were away.

Individual Activity

Hand out the activity page to each student, and allow five or ten minutes to complete it.

ACTIVITY: "In Three Years, I'd Like to Be Living..."

Where would you like to be living in three years? Use the space below to describe the situation: living with parents or on your own, in an apartment or house, sharing with roommates or living alone, etc. State whether or not you think your ambitions are realistic. Also, note any problems you foresee which might prevent you from achieving your ambitions.

Why Are Young People Homeless?

- Parents may split up and sell the family home once the children are grown up. Children over eighteen who were living at home might find that they have nowhere to stay.

- Trouble with parents and/or brothers and sisters is often a reason why young people leave home. They may become homeless before they have a chance to find alternative accommodation.

- Inability or refusal to work or receive welfare is another cause for homelessness.

- Most young people who live outside the family home are in private rented accommodation. If they fall behind with the rent—and statistics suggest that debt is a serious problem for many young people today—the landlord may take action to evict them from the property.

- Drugs may cause of homelessness if a person decides to forsake the costs of accommodation in order to spend money to support his/her drug habit.

- They are kicked out of their homes by their parents.

Small Group Activity

Ask the class to form small groups. Hand out the activity page and allow about fifteen minutes to complete it. Invite the small groups to share their answers with the large group.

ACTIVITY: Living on Your Own

1. Give three reasons why a young person might leave home even though he/she has nowhere else to live.

2. Why might someone who is unemployed have difficulty finding suitable housing? Give two reasons.

3. Some landlords are reluctant to rent apartments or houses to students. Give two reasons why.

4. Give two reasons why a young person might fall behind with his/her rent.

Other Problems Related to Homelessness

Not having anywhere permanent to stay is usually only one of many problems a person faces once he/she become homeless.

- If a person lives on the street, it is difficult to find employment because he/she has no fixed address where he/she can be contacted. Even if a person lives in a shelter, some employers may be reluctant to offer a job because they think the person's homeless status might lead to unreliability.

- Homeless people are vulnerable to exploitation by unscrupulous landlords who offer accommodation but charge very high rent. The accommodation may also be of poor quality.

- Young people living on the street are often approached by criminals who try to supply them with drugs or encourage them to become involved in illegal activities such as drug dealing, theft, and prostitution.

- People living on the streets are often the subjects of violent attacks by gangs or other homeless people.

- Living on the streets or in poor housing can make it difficult to hold down a job or to study effectively for examinations.

- Figures show that homeless people are much more likely to suffer from bad health and psychological problems.

Small Group Case Study

Ask the class to form small groups, and hand out the case study to each group. Allow about ten minutes to complete it, then invite the small groups to share their lists with the class. Compile a whole-group list. Each small group should then select from that list three of the most realistic (in their opinion) explanations of what might have happened to John to change his life so dramatically.

CASE STUDY: John

Background Information

When he graduated from school at seventeen, John was living with his parents in a small town north of San Francisco Bay. He got a good job in a bank and started saving to move into a flat of his own in San Francisco. However, just two years later, John was living on the streets in San Francisco, with no money and no job.

Discuss

What might have happened to cause such a change in John's life between the ages of seventeen and nineteen? Use the space below to make a list of reasons which might explain why John left his parents' home and is now homeless.

After the whole-group list has been compiled, select the three reasons which provide the most realistic explanations (in your opinion) of what have happened to John to change his life so dramatically. Be prepared to explain your choices.

How to Avoid Becoming Homeless

- Don't move out of your parents' home until you have arranged suitable alternative housing.

- If you are renting a room, apartment, or house, make sure you know your rights as a tenant.

- If you think you might lose your home, seek advice immediately.

- Don't decide to leave your parents' home without being absolutely sure that this is what you want. Be realistic—the accommodation at home might not be perfect, but it may be better than anything else you could afford.

- If you are leaving home to study at a university or college, make arrangements for housing as early as possible. If you leave it to the last minute, you may have nowhere to stay for the first term or longer.

- If you are renting a place, don't overstretch yourself financially. A good rule to follow is that your rent bill should account for no more than a quarter of what you earn each or month. If it costs more than this, you may find yourself struggling to pay it.

- If you have to leave home but cannot afford to rent a place of your own, consider sharing an apartment or house, renting a room, or living with another family.

Individual Activity

Hand out the activity page to each student and allow about ten minutes to complete it. Then invite the students to share their suggestions.

ACTIVITY: Student Housing Shortage

In your city, there is a shortage of affordable, suitable housing for college students. In the space below, write a letter to either the student housing office or the city council, explaining what the problem is and offering three suggestions about what might be done to improve the situation.

Small Group Case Study

Ask the class to form small groups and hand out the case study to each group. Allow about thirty minutes to complete it, then invite the group to share their answers with the large group.

CASE STUDY: Paula

Background Information

Paula ran away from home when she was fourteen to get away from her father, who she claimed had sexually abused her. She bought a bus ticket to Dallas and planned to rent a room while she searched for work. When she arrived in Dallas, a couple of girls who were renting an apartment approached her. They said she could stay with them for free. Paula accepted the offer. Soon she regretted her decision because, although she didn't have to pay rent, the other girls made her pay for all their food and cigarettes. After a couple of weeks, Paula's money was gone. The other girls didn't want her around anymore, so they locked her out of the apartment and threw her possessions out on the street.

Paula spent the next three months living in a series of homeless shelters. Sometimes she was forced to sleep on the street because there were no beds available in the shelters. Then she was offered a permanent room in a shelter run by a charity. However, her parents discovered she was living there and came to Dallas to persuade her to return home.

Paula was scared that if she stayed in the shelter her parents would use the law to force her to go home with them. A boy and a friend of his who lived in the same shelter said they knew a place Paula could stay where her parents would never find her. Paula hesitated but eventually accepted.

She found herself living in a house occupied by prostitutes, and the guy who had arranged for her to stay there started pressuring her to sleep with men for money. Paula refused at first, but she had no money for food. Because she had started taking drugs when she lived with the first two girls in the apartment, the guy offered to supply a fix whenever she wanted if she did what he asked.

Paula was found slumped on the steps outside the house a couple of months later. A passer-by called an ambulance, but she died on the way to the hospital. She had overdosed on sleeping pills. There was no suicide note, but it seemed that she intended to take her own life.

CASE STUDY: Paula (page 2)

Discussion Questions

1. Because Paula was homeless, she was an easy target for other people to exploit. Give two examples of how other people took advantage of Paula.

2. Why do you think Paula started taking drugs after she had been in Dallas a few weeks?

3. What pressures led Paula to become a prostitute?

4. Paula ran away from home because of the trouble with her father. Suggest two ways Paula could have dealt with the problem with her father without having to run away.

5. What can be done to help young people like Paula who are homeless? Give two practical suggestions.

6. What happened to Paula could happen to any young person, male or female. Do you agree with this statement? Why or why not?

Hand out the activity to each student, and allow about ten minutes to complete it. Then invite the class to share their answers.

ACTIVITY: "If I Were Homeless..."

Imagine that it is winter and you are living on the streets in a big city. In the space below, explain how you would keep warm, healthy, and clean and how you would get money and food.

Small Group Role-Play

Ask the class to form groups of four, then hand out the role-play to each group. Allow fifteen minutes for them to create both role-plays. Decide whether you want each group to present one or both versions.

Afterward, lead a group discussion based on the following questions:

- Why do landlords and tenants sometimes disagree?
- What can young renters do to avoid such disagreements? Should they not play loud music or have late-night parties, or would such restrictions be oppressive?

ROLE-PLAY: Party On or Party Off?

Background Information

Three young people are renting a house. They have had a couple of parties recently, which were rather noisy and lasted all night. The next-door neighbor, an elderly woman, has complained to their landlord, who has come over to discuss the matter with his tenants.

Three-Minute Role-Play

Decide who will play the three tenants and the landlord. Create a role-play; pick up the scene with both sides being obstinate and refusing to see the other's point of view. The discussion should become heated, with the landlord eventually threatening to evict the young people if they have any more parties.

Then do a second role-play. This time, both sides should make an effort to settle their differences so that the landlord and the neighbor are satisfied that the problem has been solved.

9 Problems at Work

Before presenting this section, read over and decide which activities, role-plays, and/or case studies your class will do. Have photocopies of the selected pages ready to hand out.

For most young people, starting work is an exciting and positive experience. A job presents fresh challenges and the opportunity to make new friends. Most problems tend to be minor and can be overcome. In a few sad cases, though, things can go seriously wrong at work so that a young person's happiness and personal well-being are threatened:

- abuse by other workers or by managers—this can be physical, verbal, or sexual abuse
- exploitation by employers or other workers
- unacceptable danger to health and safety
- encouragement from other workers or employers to break the law

Though these problems can affect anyone, some groups of workers are more vulnerable than others. Young people just starting work fall into this category. Sometimes older people in the workplace take advantage of younger workers, exploiting their youth and inexperience.

Individual Activity

Hand out the activity to each student, and allow about thirty minutes to complete it.

ACTIVITY: Abuse in the Workplace

Write a short story about a young person who is being physically, verbally, or sexually abused at work. Explain what the abuse involves and what effect it has on the young person. Use the back of this page if you need more space.

Know about Employee Rights

Workers should know their rights. Workers don't have to put up with abuse from other workers or managers. No matter what a person's position in the company, he/she is entitled to be treated with respect. All workers have grounds for filing complaints if they are ever subject to physical, verbal, or sexual abuse.

Sometimes, though, it is difficult to define "abuse." For example, if a male worker puts his arm around the shoulder of a female colleague, it may just be a friendly gesture—he may do the same thing with male colleagues—but it could also be an uninvited sexual advance. Another example of abuse in the workplace would be if one worker called another worker "Guido" because he has Italian parents. The workers might mean this to be just a friendly nickname, but the subject of the "friendliness" may take offense..

If workers find themselves in an uncomfortable position in the workplace, they should remember:

- No one must tolerate anyone at work calling names or invading personal space.

- Employees are within their rights when they politely but firmly tell the person calling names or making inappropriate gestures to stop. If the person ignores the request and continues, the offended workers are also within their rights to complain to the employer, trade union, or even the police if necessary.

Ultimately, it is up to the person being harassed to decide what action, if any, to take. Here are some suggestions:

- If you get upset by the way you are being treated at work, but think you might be over-reacting, talk to people in whom you can confide—parents, friends, former teachers, people you get along with at work, etc.—and ask their opinion.

- Try to anticipate and avoid situations where you might be at risk of abuse from people you work with. For example, it would be unwise to accept a lift home from a colleague who you believe has been making unwanted sexual advances toward you or other people at work.

- If you are not the only person in the workplace who believes they are being mistreated, complain together, as there is strength in numbers. If you are the only person who is being abused, don't let this stop you from making a complaint.

- If you have participated in verbal, sexual, or physical abuse of others in the past, it will be hard to complain if you suddenly become a victim of abuse yourself. Treat other workers with the same kindness and respect that you would expect from them.

- Don't be put off because people give you a hard time for making a complaint against them.

Small Group Case Study

Ask the class to form small groups and hand out the following case study to each group. Allow about twenty minutes to complete it. Then invite the small groups to share their answers with the large group.

CASE STUDY: Jenny, James, and Lianne

Background Information

Case #1: Jenny is a shop assistant at a lumberyard. Every morning when she arrives at work, the guys in the yard who load the trucks whistle in her direction and ask if she has a boyfriend and whether she would go out with them.

Case #2: There is a partner in the firm Joe works for who really makes him mad. He calls Joe "gingernut" because of the color of his hair. No one else in the firm calls him this name.

Case #3: Lianne works in a museum. She was playing around with one of her co-workers when she accidentally knocked over an antique porcelain vase. The vase broke into hundreds of pieces and her boss had a fit. She accused Lianne of being careless and stupid and at one stage shook her by the shoulders aggressively.

Discussion Questions

1. In each case, would the person concerned be justified in complaining about the way he/she is being treated?

2. Why might Jenny be upset by the behavior of the guys who load the trucks?

CASE STUDY: Jenny, James, and Lianne (page 2)

3. Joe makes an appointment to meet the partner who calls him "gingernut." He intends to ask him to stop calling him this name. What arguments might Joe make in order to get the partner to see things from his point of view?

4. It was Lianne's fault that the vase broke, but she thinks her boss over-reacted. How do you think her boss should have reacted?

5. Lianne doesn't intend to be physically abused by her boss again, though she is not prepared to leave her job. What should Lianne say to her boss to make it clear that she won't stand for being physically attacked?

Street Smarts © 1995 Resource Publications, Inc.

Exploitation in the Workplace

Today children are protected from exploitation in the workplace by federal and state laws. In most cases, federal law prohibits employing children under the age of fourteen. A person who is at least sixteen years old may be employed in most non-hazardous jobs. They may work no more than three hours on a school day and no more than eighteen hours in a school week.

Although such regulations are in place, exploitation of youth can still happen. Examples include:

- very low pay, i.e., wages below a level compatible with human dignity
- less wages for young people performing the same job as older workers
- dangerous conditions
- pressure to take part in unethical commercial activities such as high-pressure selling
- older workers loading some of the work they should be doing onto younger workers

Some forms of exploitation are illegal; others are immoral without necessarily breaking the law. Often it is difficult to prove that employers are exploiting their workers. Unscrupulous employers thrive in situations where their workers are inexperienced and unsure of their rights. Workers can avoid being exploited by taking some sensible precautions.

Investigate the Company's Reputation First

Before accepting a job, check out the company. Job searchers should know the answers to the following questions:

- Does this company have a good reputation as an employer in the area?
- Has it been in business long?
- Does it make suitable arrangements for training young workers?

Job searchers can find out the answers by asking anyone who works for the company or who has friends or relatives who work for the company. Community or campus career centers can provide job searchers with information as well.

Know the Terms and Conditions of Employment

Once hired, the terms and conditions should be outlined in a work contract, an agreement between the worker and employer. It sets out details such as hours of work, vacation periods, health benefits, rate of pay, arrangements for overtime, place of employment, job description, etc. Employers are not allowed to change the terms and conditions of employment without the worker's permission.

Report Poor Treatment

If other workers try to exploit another worker in some way, the worker should complain in the first instance to a manager. If nothing is done about it, the worker should take his/her complaint higher up or contact a trade union official (a person doesn't necessarily have to be a member of a union to ask a union official to consider a complaint).

If an employer takes advantage of a worker, the worker has a number of options. He/she can:

- arrange a meeting with the employer or the personnel manager to discuss the matter
- find out if other workers feel the same and complain together
- ask the union or workers' representative to pursue the matter
- look for another job (but it is generally not advisable to leave one's present employment until another job is secured).

If a worker complains to his/her employer and the employer responds by firing the worker, the fired employee may have a case for unlawful dismissal.

Small Group Role-Play

Ask the class to form groups of three, and hand out the role-play to each group. Allow five or ten minutes for them to create their role-play. After each group presents its role-play, lead a whole-group discussion of the following questions:

- Why do some people steal from their employers?
- What might be the consequences?

ROLE-PLAY: Employee Theft

Background Information

Trevor has been working in a car parts store for about two weeks. Four other employees work there. Trevor suspects that two of them are operating some kind of racket. His fears are confirmed when the two try to persuade him to join them in stealing parts and selling them for cash to a back-street garage.

Three-Minute Role-Play

Decide who will play Trevor and the two dishonest employees. Pick up the scene in which the two are persuading Trevor to join them. What might they say to tempt him? What threats might they make if he refuses? Trevor should stay calm and give reasons why he will not break the law and risk his job. He should also try to convince the others to stop their involvement.

Small Group Case Study

Ask the class to form small groups, and hand out the case study to each group. Allow about fifteen minutes to complete it. Then invite the small groups to share their recommendations with the whole group.

CASE STUDY: Tracy

Background Information

Tracy is eighteen and works as a kitchen assistant in a posh restaurant. She was earning $7/hour and having a hard time living on that wage. Now she has been asked to accept a wage cut to $6/hour because the restaurant has not been very busy lately. Tracy can't afford to live on such a low wage. She is mad, too, because she knows that last week the manager offered the head chef a big raise to stop him from going to work for another restaurant. Tracy thinks the manager is taking advantage of her because she is young and he knows she won't find it easy to get another job elsewhere.

Your Recommendations to Tracy

Here is a list of Tracy's options. Check the boxes below based on whether you would recommend or not recommend each option. Be prepared to explain your recommendation to the whole group.

- Complain to the restaurant owners. ☐ Recommended ☐ Not Recommended
- Threaten to go on strike. ☐ Recommended ☐ Not Recommended
- Accept the pay cut without saying anything. ☐ Recommended ☐ Not Recommended
- Accept the pay cut but sabotage some of the restaurant meals for revenge. ☐ Recommended ☐ Not Recommended
- Quit and hope to find work elsewhere. ☐ Recommended ☐ Not Recommended
- Tell the manager that she has been offered another job which will pay her $6.50 an hour. ☐ Recommended ☐ Not Recommended

Resources for Further Study

CONSUMER ISSUES

Campbell, Roger F., Sr. *The Better Business Bureau A to Z Buying Guide*. New York: Henry Holt, 1990.

Eiler, Andrew. *The Consumer Protection Manual*. New York: Facts on File Publications, 1984.

Leski, Matthew. *The Great American Gripe Book*. Kensington, Maryland: Information USA, Inc. 1991.

CULTS

Galanter, Marc. *Cults: Faith, Healing, and Coercion*. New York: Oxford University Press, 1989.

Melton, J. Gordon. *Encyclopedic Handbook of Cults in America*. New York: Garland Publishing, 1992.

Streissguth, Thomas. *Charismatic Cult Leaders*. Minneapolis: Oliver Press 1995.

DELINQUENCY

Biskup, Michael D. *Youth Violence*. San Diego: Greenhaven Press, 1992.

Kramer, Rita. *At a Tender Age: Violent Youth and Juvenile Justice*. New York: Henry Holt, 1988.

Sander, Daryl. *Focus on Teens in Trouble: A Reference Handbook*. Santa Barbara, California: ABC-CLIO, 1991.

DRUGS

Berger, Gilda. *Joey's Story: Get Real! Straight Talk about Drugs*. Brookfield, Connecticut: Millbrook Press, 1991.

McCormick, Michele. *Designer Drug Abuse*. New York: F. Watts, 1989.

Truck, Mary. *Crack and Cocaine*. New York: Crestwood House, 1990.

GANGS

Greenburg, Keith Elliot. *Out of the Gang*. Minneapolis: Lerner Publications, 1992.

Miller, Maryann. *Coping with Weapons and Violence in Your School and on Your Streets*. New York: Rosen Publishing Group, 1993.

Webb, Margot. *Coping with Street Gangs*. New York: Rosen Publishing Group, 1990.

HOMELESSNESS

Coates, Robert C. *A Street Is Not a Home: Solving America's Homeless Dilemma*. Buffalo: Prometheus Books, 1990.

Homeless, Joe. *My Life on the Street: Memoirs of a Faceless Man*. Far Hills, New York: New Horizon Press, 1994.

Snow, David, and Leon Anderson. *Down on Their Luck: A Study of Homeless Street People*. Berkeley: University of California Press, 1993.

PROBLEMS AT WORK

Carrier, Lois, Bill Gooch, and John Huck. *Work: Pathway to Independence*. Chicago: American Technological Society, 1979.

Douglass, Merrill E., and Donna Douglass. *Manage Your Time, Your Work, Yourself*. New York: AMA-COM, 1993.

Langela, Martha. *Back Off*. New York: Simon and Schuster, 1993.

Radin, Bill. *Take This Job and Leave It*. Hawthorn, New Jersey: Career Press, 1993.

SEXUAL EXPLOITATION

Bass, Ellen. *The Courage to Heal: A Guide for Women Survivors of Child Sexual Abuse*. New York: Perennial Library, 1990.

Gordon, Thomas. *Enslaved*. New York: Pharos Books, 1991.

Landau, Elaine. *On the Streets: The Lives of Adolescent Prostitutes*. New York: Simon and Schuster, 1987.

STREET VIOLENCE

Barden, Renardo. *Juvenile Violence*. North Bellmore, New York: M. Cavendish, 1994.

Schorr, Lisbeth, and Daniel Schorr. *Within Our Reach: Breaking the Cycle of Disadvantage*. New York: Doubleday, 1988.

Silberman, Charles E. *Criminal Violence, Criminal Justice*. New York: Random House, Vintage Books, 1980.

More Resources for Helping Teens Take Care of Themselves

FACING VIOLENCE: Discussion-Starting Skits for Teenagers

R. William Pike

Paper, $19.95, 192 pages, 6" x 9", ISBN 0-89390-344-2

Teens have many reasons for acting up. Trouble at home. Trouble with relationships. Trouble on the streets. You can get them to talk about their problems and explore solutions by using simple dramas. *Facing Violence*, part of the *Acting It Out* series, provides you with 40 skits addressing violence in schools, violence in the home, violent language, violence and dating, violence and bias, violence in society—and solutions. Try them. They work!

SO, WHAT IS ASSERTIVENESS? An Assertiveness Training Course

Chrissie Whitehead

Paper, $29.95, 64 pages, 8½" x 11", ISBN 0-89390-296-9

Aggressive vs. Assertive. What's the difference? This book clarifies the difference between assertive and aggressive behavior, emphasizing that assertive behavior brings about acceptable results to all involved. Educators will appreciate the easy-to-use lesson plans and **photocopiable** handouts which lead to identifying and changing patterns of aggressive behavior. The lessons can be taught as a separate course, worked into a self-esteem or life-skills course, or used in less structured situations in youth or neighborhood groups, teacher in-services, adult education programs, or business offices. Based on a version published by Daniels Publishing, Cambridge, England, *So, What Is Assertiveness?* was revised and edited especially for use in North America.

ACTING IT OUT: 74 Short Plays for Starting Discussions with Teenagers

Joan Sturkie & Marsh Cassady, PhD

Paper, $21.95, 358 pages, 6" x 9", ISBN 0-89390-178-4

Getting teens to talk about their feelings and personal experiences can be frustrating. *Acting It Out* offers a new approach: Teens act out a short play, then discuss how the characters deal with the particular issue. Questions at the end of each drama will help students articulate issues and feelings. These dramas address challenging subjects: abortion, suicide, child abuse, gangs, anorexia, home life, drugs, and more. Issues are presented in a straightforward manner; your teens are encouraged to talk about them in the same way.

FISHING FOR VALUES:
Card Games and Exercises for Identifying Personal and Life Values

Astrid Berg

2 card decks boxed with 32-page instruction booklet, $15, ISBN 0-89390-294-2

When students participate in *Fishing for Values* games and exercises, they take an active part in forming who they are and what they believe as individuals. Such self-directed activity helps participants understand that the values they name and own are theirs, not something they have inherited or memorized. Useful for teens through adults. The instruction booklet contains a master values list and rules for twelve different games and exercises.

Order from your local bookseller, or use the order form on the last page.

THE PEER HELPER'S POCKETBOOK

Joan Sturkie & Valerie Gibson

Paper, $7.95, 104 pages, 4" x 7"
ISBN 0-89390-237-3

This small book has proven helpful in both empowering and instructing students. It has come to symbolize responsible peer helping among students everywhere. *The Peer Helper's Pocketbook* is a quick and easy guide written for peer helpers/counselors on the junior and senior high school as well as college levels. Everything needed for effective peer support is here: review of basic communication skills, counseling tips, synopsis of information on issues, and a section for important referral telephone numbers—for those times when more help is indicated. Put a copy in the faculty room, too, because it is a handy reference for faculty, counselors, and parents.

THE PEER HELPING TRAINING COURSE

Joan Sturkie & Maggie Phillips

3-ring binder holding 280 pages with section tabs, $54.95, 8½" x 11", ISBN 0-89390-311-6

Revised and Expanded Edition!

This revised and expanded version of *The Peer Counseling Training Course* is a complete curriculum and teacher's guide for a high school course, which can also be used with some junior high school students.

Because teenagers find it easier to talk about their problems with each other, you need a resource that teaches students how to help their peers identify and talk about their issues and feelings. *The Peer Helping Training Course* helps teens learn how to be there for each other in a positive way. Part I (units 1-9) introduces the skills students need to be good communicators. Part II (units 10-23) deals with specific problems such as peer pressure, drugs, death, AIDS. Revised edition contains four new chapters addressing cultural diversity, violence, depression, and belonging and empowerment. Appendices contain a sample letter to parents of peer helpers, glossary, community resources, and an excellent bibliography.

er Helping Training Course
The Peer Helping Training Course The Peer Helping **Peer** Helping Training Course The Peer Helping Training Course The Peer Helping Training Course T he Peer Helping Training C **Training** Course The Peer elping Training Course Th **Course** The Peer Helping aining Course The Peer H

Joan Sturkie
Maggie Phillips

Order Form

Order these resources from your local bookstore, or mail this form to:

 Resource Publications, Inc.
160 E. Virginia Street #290 - SS
San Jose, CA 95112-5876
(408) 286-8505
(408) 287-8748 FAX

QTY	TITLE	PRICE	TOTAL

Subtotal: _____

CA residents add 7¼% sales tax
(Santa Clara Co. residents, 8¼%): _____

Postage and handling
($3 for order up to $30; 10% of order over $30 but less than $150; $15 for order of $150 or more): _____

Total: _____

☐ My check or money order is enclosed.
☐ Charge my ☐ VISA ☐ MC.

Expiration Date _____

Card # _____ - _____ - _____ - _____

Signature _____

Name (print) _____

Institution_____

Street _____

City/State/ZIP _____